HANDS-ON DATA ENGINEERING

From Zero to Production

Nitin Rane

CONTENTS

INTRODUCTION

I ntroduction: Data Engineering – From Zero to Production
Welcome to Hands-On Data Engineering: From Zero to Production, your practical guide to building real-world data pipelines. This book isn't about abstract theory; it's a hands-on journey that takes you from foundational concepts to implementing a fully functional, production-ready data engineering project.

Why This Book?

In today's data-driven world, effective data engineering is the backbone of any successful organization. The ability to collect, store, transform, and analyze data at scale is crucial for gaining a competitive edge, making informed decisions, and driving innovation. This book bridges the gap between theoretical knowledge and practical skills, equipping you with the expertise to design, build, and manage robust data pipelines.

What You'll Learn

By the end of this book, you'll be able to:

Understand the Fundamentals: Grasp core data engineering principles, including data collection, storage architectures (Data Lakes, Data Warehouses, and Lakehouses), and ETL processes.

Understand Essential Technologies: Gain hands-on experience

with Python, Apache Airflow, and a range of popular databases:

MSSQL: For transactional data and enterprise-level integrations.

PostgreSQL: For analytical workloads and as a staging database.

MySQL: For lightweight and quick data storage needs.

BigQuery: For scalable, serverless data warehousing in the cloud.

Build Scalable Data Pipelines: Design and implement data pipelines capable of handling thousands of tasks using Apache Airflow and Python.

Tackle Real-World Challenges: Address memory constraints when dealing with large datasets, build incremental pipelines, and design pipelines for different data synchronization scenarios.

Construct a Common Framework: Develop robust, reusable, and scalable data synchronization frameworks to automate and speed up pipeline development.

Who This Book Is For

This book is for anyone who wants to become a proficient data engineer. Whether you're a software engineer, data scientist, or IT professional looking to expand your skillset, this book will provide you with the knowledge and practical experience you need to succeed. No prior data engineering experience is required.

Embark on Your Data Engineering Journey

Get ready to roll up your sleeves and dive into the world of data engineering. Let's begin building your journey from zero to production.

If you want to setup your project or need support then i am reachable on idmreq@gmail.com

1. GETTING STARTED WITH DATA ENGINEERING

What Is Data Engineering?

Data engineering involves designing and building systems that collect, store, and process large volumes of data. It forms the backbone of modern data-driven organizations, enabling analytics, machine learning, and other applications.

Data engineering is a specialized field that bridges the gap between raw data and actionable insights. Data engineers are responsible for building and maintaining the robust infrastructure that supports data-driven decision-making. They design, develop, and manage the systems that collect, store, transform, and prepare data for analysis.

As a data engineer, your responsibilities include:
- Creating robust data pipelines to move and trans form data.
- Optimizing systems for scalability and reliability.
- Collaborating with data scientists and analysts to deliver actionable insights.

Data Engineering: The Backbone Of Data-Driven

Decisions.

Data engineering is a specialized field that bridges the gap between raw data and actionable insights. Data engineers are responsible for building and maintaining the robust infrastructure that supports data-driven decision-making. They design, develop, and manage the systems that collect, store, transform, and prepare data for analysis.

Key Responsibilities of Data Engineers:

- Data Collection: Gathering data from various sources, including databases, APIs, sensors, and logs.

- Data Storage: Designing and managing storage solutions, such as data warehouses, data lakes, and databases, to ensure efficient retrieval and processing.

- Data Processing: Building and maintaining data pipelines to transform raw data into a usable format for analysis. This involves tasks like data cleaning, transformation, and integration.

- Data Quality: Ensuring the accuracy, completeness, and consistency of data throughout the entire lifecycle.

- Data Security: Implementing security measures to protect sensitive data from unauthorized access and breaches.

- Data Governance: Establishing and enforcing policies and procedures for data management and usage.

Tools and Technologies Used by Data Engineers:
- **Programming Languages:** Python, Java, Scala, SQL
- **Big Data Technologies:** Hadoop, Spark, Kafka
- **Cloud Platforms:** AWS, Azure, GCP
- **Data Warehousing:** Snowflake, Redshift, BigQuery
- **Data Pipelines:** Apache Airflow, Luigi, Prefect
- **Data Visualization:** Tableau, Power BI

The Importance Of Data Engineering

In today's data-driven world, data engineering plays a critical role in enabling businesses to gain a competitive advantage. By providing high-quality, accessible data, data engineers empower data scientists, analysts, and business users to make informed decisions and drive innovation.

In this book, you'll step into the shoes of a data engineer, learning how to solve practical challenges and build systems that work at scale.

2. DATA STORAGE ARCHITECTURES

Data Lake, Lakehouse, and
Data Warehouse

What Are Data Storage Architectures?

In data engineering, choosing the right storage architecture is crucial. Each architecture is designed to serve different needs based on data volume, variety, velocity, and access patterns.

1. Data Lake

- Definition: A centralized repository that allows you to store all your structured, semi-structured, and unstructured data at any scale.
- Key Features:
    - Schema-on-read
    - High scalability and low-cost storage
    - Suitable for big data and analytics workloads

- Use Case:
    - Data lakes are ideal for storing raw data from multiple sources for future processing.

Hands-On:

- Set up an Amazon S3 bucket or a Hadoop Distributed File System (HDFS) as your data lake.
- Ingest raw data from PostgreSQL into the data lake.

2. Data Warehouse

- Definition: A storage system optimized for querying and analyzing structured data, typically using SQL.
- Key Features:
  - Schema-on-write
  - High performance for analytical queries
  - Suitable for business intelligence and reporting
- Use Case:
  - Data warehouses are best for historical and current reporting.

Hands-On:

- Configure Google BigQuery as a data warehouse.
- Load aggregated data from the PostgreSQL staging area.

3. Lakehouse

- Definition: A hybrid approach combining the scalability and flexibility of data lakes with the structure and query optimization of data warehouses.
- Key Features:
  - Supports ACID transactions
  - Unified storage and analytics
  - Reduces data duplication
- Use Case:
  - Lakehouses are suitable for real-time analytics and

machine learning workloads.

Hands-On:

- Use Apache Delta Lake or Databricks to implement a lakehouse architecture.
- Build a real-time pipeline syncing data from MSSQL to the lakehouse.

Comparison Table

Feature	Data Lake	Data Warehouse	Lakehouse
Data Type	Structured, Semi-structured, Unstructured	Structured	Structured, Semi-structured
Schema	Schema-on-read	Schema-on-write	Schema-on-read + ACID
Use Cases	Big Data Analytics	Business Intelligence	Real-time ML Analytics
Cost Efficiency	High	Moderate to High	Moderate
Query Performance	Moderate	High	High

When To Use What?

- Data Lake: When dealing with raw data or requiring a scalable storage solution for diverse data types.
- Data Warehouse: When the focus is on structured data analytics and reporting.
- Lakehouse: When requiring the flexibility of a data lake combined with analytical capabilities.

In this book we are going to deal with a data warehouse with Bigquery as data storage.

3. SETTING UP YOUR ENVIRONMENT

To get started, you'll need to set up your environment with the tools and technologies required throughout this book.

Tools And Technologies:

- **Python**: The primary language for scripting and building pipelines.
- **Apache Airflow**: A workflow orchestration tool to automate your pipelines.
- **Databases**: MSSQL, PostgreSQL, MySQL, and BigQuery for storage and processing.

Installation Guide:

1. **Python**:

- Download and install Python 3.10 or later from python.org.
- Verify installation:

  python --version
  pip --version

2. **Apache Airflow**:

- Install Airflow using pip:

  pip install apache-airflow

- Initialize the Airflow database:

  airflow db init

- Start the Airflow web server:

airflow webserver

3. **Databases**:

- Install database clients (e.g., psycopg2 for PostgreSQL).
- Set up access credentials for MSSQL, MySQL, and BigQuery.

To build a robust data engineering environment, we'll start by setting up and populating the databases:

1. **Install and Configure Databases**:

- Install MSSQL, PostgreSQL, and MySQL on your local system or use cloud-hosted versions.
- Set up a BigQuery project in Google Cloud.

2. **Create Sample Tables**: Each database will have a sample table with varying data types (e.g., integers, strings, dates, booleans).

Example: Creating a Table in PostgreSQL:

```
CREATE TABLE employee (
    employee_id SERIAL PRIMARY KEY,
    first_name VARCHAR(50),
    last_name VARCHAR(50),
    hire_date DATE,
    salary NUMERIC(10, 2),
    is_active BOOLEAN
);
```

3. **Populate Data**: Populate each table with approximately 10 million records to simulate real-world scenarios.

Example: Populating Data in PostgreSQL:

```
INSERT INTO employee (first_name, last_name, hire_date, salary, is_active)
```

```
SELECT
   'FirstName' || generate_series(1, 10000),
   'LastName' || generate_series(1, 10000),
   CURRENT_DATE - (random() * 365)::int,
   (random() * 1000)::numeric(10, 2),
   (random() > 0.5)::boolean
FROM generate_series(1, 10000);
```

Repeat similar steps for MSSQL and MySQL, adjusting syntax as needed.

4. **Verify Data**: Query the tables to ensure the data is populated correctly:

4. BUILDING YOUR FIRST DATA PIPELINE

Understanding Data Pipelines

A data pipeline is a series of processes that move data from a source to a destination, transforming it along the way to make it usable.
In this chapter, we'll focus on a batch processing pipeline and take you through building one using Python.

Hands-On: Creating A Basic Etl Pipeline

ETL stands for Extract, Transform, and Load—the core steps of most data pipelines:

1. **Extract**: Fetching data from a source.
2. **Transform**: Cleaning, enriching, and reshaping data for analysis.
3. **Load**: Saving the transformed data into a destination.

Step 1: Extract Data

We'll use Python's libraries to connect to a database and extract data.

Example: Extracting Data from PostgreSQL

```python
import psycopg2

def extract_data():
    conn = psycopg2.connect(
        dbname="your_database",
        user="your_username",
        password="your_password",
        host="localhost",
        port="5432"
    )
    cursor = conn.cursor()
    cursor.execute("SELECT * FROM employee LIMIT 1000;")
    data = cursor.fetchall()
    cursor.close()
    conn.close()
    return data
```

◆ ◆ ◆

Step 2: Transform Data

Transform data is optional, we may not have to do it always.

Transformations can include:
- Data type conversions
- Removing duplicates
- Aggregations or calculations

Example: Transforming Extracted Data

```
def transform_data(data):
    transformed_data = []
    for record in data:
        full_name = f"{record[1]} {record[2]}"
        salary_in_k = record[4] / 1000   # Convert salary to thousands
        transformed_data.append((record[0], full_name, salary_in_k, record[5]))
    return transformed_data
```

Step 3: Load Data

The transformed data will be inserted into another database or storage system.

Example: Loading Data into MySQL

```
def load_data(data):
    conn = mysql.connector.connect(
        host="localhost",
        user="your_username",
        password="your_password",
        database="your_database"
    )
    cursor = conn.cursor()
    insert_query = """
        INSERT INTO transformed_employee (employee_id, full_name, salary_in_k, is_active)
        VALUES (%s, %s, %s, %s)
    """
    cursor.executemany(insert_query, data)
    conn.commit()
    cursor.close()
    conn.close()
```

Step 4: Combine Etl Steps

Here's how we can combine all the steps to create a simple pipeline:

```python
if __name__ == "__main__":
    extracted_data = extract_data()
    transformed_data = transform_data(extracted_data)
    load_data(transformed_data)
    print("ETL pipeline executed successfully!")
```

Run this script to execute the pipeline manually.

5. DESIGNING FOR SCALE

Now that we have developed a basic pipeline let's move further to understand how to build real world pipelines. The data pipeline tasks are repetitive, meaning most of the tasks will look similar, so it is better to create a common framework to automate and speed up development of the data pipeline tasks.

Let's start building our common framework which will handle data at scale.

Scenarios

We will build below data pipeline scenarios, which covers pretty much everything required for the production environment.

1. To build a data pipeline we have scenarios like data to be synced every minute, 5 minute, likewise, it could be hourly, every hour or 3 hours, once in a day and we have to make sure it is incremental.

The data sync should begin from where it finished the last sync.

2. Full sync, backfill, sometimes due to some changes in the source we may have to **backfill** data from the past.When we move certain table to data warehouse we have to first do a **full sync**

3.Insert new records and update existing records in the target (Upsert)

4.Insert only - only insert records into the target

5.Delete the records of the target and insert

17

The request comes from different teams like, analytics or reports team when they need certain table in data warehouse/lake

As analytics and reports processing requires heavy computations it is not advisable to do it with live DBs so we move data from live DB to data warehouse/lake built in big data technologies.

When we build a data warehouse/lake we move tables to bigquery or redshift or other similar big data platforms.

When we move a table for the first time we have to do full sync and then regularly merge live data in the data warehouse/lake.

When we move full table to data warehouse there could be significant challenges due to limited computing resources, like RAM

So while building a data pipeline and moving the full table to the data warehouse/lake we may encounter memory issues.

Handling Memory Issues

N ow assume the employee table which we populated above has 70 million records totaling about 8 GB or more in size.

Assume the machine where we run the pipeline has 4 GB of RAM.

So in this case when we execute a select query to do full sync the records from the table being more in size than the RAM size will cause out of memory and the pipeline will never succeed.

So let's first handle this scenario.

When we start syncing data from source to a target table we have to make sure that all the records are not fetched at a time to ensure we do not run out of RAM.

To achieve this we need to stream the data from the database.

Sqlachemy connection provides us with the option to stream the data.

- •Streaming Enables the database connection to stream results row by row (or in chunks) instead of fetching all rows at once.
- •Useful for queries that return a large number of rows, as it prevents excessive memory usage.

Streaming characteristics are as below

- **Lower Memory Usage**:
  - Since results are fetched incrementally, you don't load the entire result set into memory at once.
- **Iterative Access**:
  - Query results are accessed one row (or a chunk of rows) at a time via an iterator.
- **Streaming Behavior**:
  - Particularly useful for use cases like writing large datasets to a file or processing records iteratively in chunks.

When we stream the data all the rows are not fetched at once but are fetched in chunks,we have to provide the chunk size to fetch the data.

If we give a chunk size as 100k then the entire table will be fetched in iterations for 100k each.

The iterations will continue until the entire table is fetched.

As only 100k records are fetched at a time it will not cause out of memory.

Below syntax tells sqlalchemy to stream the result

Python code

src_conn=engine.connect().execution_otions(stream_results=True)

Comparison table

Feature	execution_options(stream_results=True)	connect()
Memory Usage	Low (streams rows incrementally)	High (loads all rows into memory)
Result Fetching	Incremental (row-by-row or chunks)	All rows at once
Performance	Optimized for large datasets	Best for small datasets
Use Case	Large result sets, low memory scenarios	Small result sets, simple queries
Ease of Use	Requires iteration to fetch rows	Simpler to use directly

In the next section create a common function to create connection.

6. CONSTRUCTING A REUSABLE FRAMEWORK

D ata pipeline tasks are going to repeatative, all of them will look almost similar.
It will be prudent to develop a reusable framework so that we do not have to start from scratch for new data pipelines.
In this reusable framework we will build a

Connection function

Define data pipeline

Data processing function

Data load function

◆ ◆ ◆

Let us start with a connection function.

Connection function

Let's build a reusable function to create connection which can handle any type of database

Python Code

```python
def get_connection(driver, connflag):
    connection_str = ""
    if (connflag == "src"):
        connection_str = _config['source_username'] + ":" + quote(_config['source_password']) + "@" + \
                        _config['source_host'] + ":" + _config['source_port'] + "/" + _config["source_db"]
    elif (connflag == "dest"):
        connection_str = _config["destination_username"] + ":" + quote(
            _config["destination_password"]) + "@" + _config["destination_host"] + ":" + \
                        _config["destination_port"] + "/" + _config["destination_db"]
    if (driver == "mysql"):
        engine = create_engine("mysql://" + connection_str)
    elif (driver == "postgresql"):
        engine = create_engine("postgres://" + connection_str)
    elif (driver == "mssql"):
        engine = create_engine("mssql+pymssql://" + connection_str)
    elif (driver == "bigquery"):
        if (connflag == "src"):
            engine = create_engine( url 'bigquery://', credentials_path=_config["gcp_key"])
        else:
            client = bigquery.Client()
            return client
    if (connflag == "src"):
        conn = engine.connect().execution_options(stream_results=True)
    else:
        conn = engine.connect()
    return conn
```

Above function creates a connection for any of the MSSql,MySQL,BigQuery,Postgres database and sets the connection as a streaming connection.

We can extend this function to include other databases.

The benefit of using sqlalchemy for connection is that it provides a wrapper so that our common framework remains unaffected by the choice of the database.

Define data pipeline

Now lets understand "_config" the variable we have used in the above function.

We define the data pipeline characteristics in the _config dictionary, it holds the details of the data pipeline as a dictionary as given below.

_config is the key to develop common framework

```
_config = {
    "metadata": ""
    "gcp_key": ""
    "schedule": ""
    "dag_id": ""
    "source_driver": ""
    "source_host": ""
    "source_port": ""
    "source_username": ""
    "source_password": ""
    "source_db": ""
    "source_schema": ""
    "source_table": ""
    "source_date_column": ""
    "selectcolumnslist": ""
    "selectcondition": ""
    "destination_driver": ""
    "date_column": ""
    "destination_host": ""
    "destination_port": ""
    "destination_schema_stg": ""
    "destination_table_stg": ""
    "destination_schema": ""
    "destination_table": ""
    "destination_username": ""
```

```
    "destination_password": ""
    "destination_keys": ""
    "insertcolumnslist": ""
    "on_duplicate": ""
    "src_dest_mapping": ""
    "fillnull": ""
    "new_columns": ""
    "default_values": ""
}
```

Let's understand the details of the _config dictionary.

metadata	information about the data pipeline
gcp_key	Path to gcp service account file, used for making connecton to BQ
Schedule	Cron expression to schedule the data pipeline
dag_id	Apache Airflow dag id, it is going to be our orchestration platform
source_driver	Type of the source database value, mysql,mssql,postgresql,bigquery. This parameter will be used in the connecton function
source_host	Data base host
source_port	Data base port to make connection, like 3306 for mysql, 1433 for mssql 5432 or 5437 for postgres etc
source_username, source_password	Credentials for connectin to the database. Not required for Bigquery as it requires service account json file
source_db	Name of the data base from where we will fetch records
source_schema	Name of the schema under the "source_db"
source_table	Name of the table from where we will read the records
select_columns	List of columns from the source table we need to fetch
destination_driver	Type of the source database value, mysql,mssql,postgresql,bigquery. This parameter will be used in the connecton function
destination_host	Data base host
destination_port	Data base port to make connection, like 3306 for mysql, 1433 for mssql 5432 or 5437 for postgres etc
destination_username, destination_password	Credentials for connectin to the database. Not required for Bigquery as it requires service account json file
destination_db	Name of the data base where we will update/ insertrecords
destination_schema	Name of the schema under the "destination_db"
destination_table	Name of the table where we will insert/update the records

insert_columns	List of columns in the targettable.
on_duplicate	If we have upsert operation then we will specify which columns to update if the record fetched from source already exists
src_dest_mapping	If the source and target column names do not match then provide the mapping of columns example {"product_id":"product_code"} this means value of column product_id in the source table need to be inserted in the product_code of the target table. Likewise we need to give mapping of all the mismatching columns
deafult_values	We may have a scenario where for certain column in target we have to fill some default value in that column while inserting .example. In default values section we provide default values {"some_column":0,"some_other_column":"current time"}
new_columns	In a scenario where some columns are not there in the source but are there in the target, so mention those columns in new_columns section along with the defult values.example {"stocktype": "1","length": 0,"width": 0}
destination_table_stg	For Bigquery, MSSql,Redshift to update existing records in batch, data is first loaded into a stage table and from stage it is merged into main table
destination_keys	We mention the primary key of the destination table. We will use this while doing upsert operation

Recap:

We have defined our data pipeline in the form of _config dictionary.

We have understood how to make connections,

we have understood how to handle data at scale.

In the next section let's enhance our common framework to

understand how to process data.

Data processing function

Fetching Data from source

As we discussed earlier in the Handling memory issues section, while fetching data we have scenarios like fetching data incrementally or fetching legacy data when we first load the table into the data warehouse.

Let's build these scenarios.

Legacy sync: Fetch entire table from source and insert into target.

Case :
We have a table employee which is still not there in the data warehouse and a request has come to load the table into the data warehouse.

As this is first time that means the entire table need to be moved to data warehouse.
So to fetch the entire table we need to start from the first record till the lastest record.

There are two ways to identify the first record,

1.If the table has auto increment ID column then the record with lowest ID would be the first record.

2.Find the minimum last modified date of the table

Using last modified date is better as it keeps track of the modifications in the records.

So the record with minimum last modified date would be the first record of the table and we must start syncing data from that date untill the latest date.

We also have to make sure that this bulk fetch operation does not overload the source database server.

If we execute select query it will load entire table into memory and we don't want that.

We can use streaming option as explained earlier but in the bulk load operation it may happen that due to some exception the sync operation fails midway.In that case we need a way too resume from where it failed.

So we will fetch data daywise, if it fails then we know on which date it failed and we can resume from there.

First we will write one function which gives us a date range from where we need to start the table sync, we will pass minimum last modified date of the table as start_date to this function.

This date range function will give us a list of every date from the minimum date in the table.

Using this date list we will be able to sync one day data so as to not overload the source DB.

Let's build the strategy.

```
def date_generator(start_date,end_date):
    step = timedelta(days=1)
    result = []

    while start_date < end_date:
        result.append(start_date.strftime('%Y-%m-%d %H:%M:%S'))
        start_date += step
    return result
```

Python Code

above function return list of date from the start_date to end_date

example

```
start_date = datetime(2023, 1, 1,0, 0, 0)
end_date = datetime(2025, 1, 5, 23, 59, 59)
date_list=date_time_list(start_date,end_date)
```

the date_list when printed will be as below
['2023-01-01 00:00:00', '2023-01-02 00:00:00', '2023-01-03 00:00:00', '2023-01-04 00:00:00'..]
and so on until what ever is the end_date passed to the function.

Next we need to use the date list in a loop as given below and generate the WHERE CONDITION dynamically.

In one iteration of a loop we fetch 1 day's data, when the loop is finished we will have completely fetched the entire table.

Python Code

```
for date_count in range(len(date_list)):
    if(date_count == len(date_list) - 1):
        condition = f" WHERE {_config['date_column']} >='{date_list[date_count]}'"
    else:
        condition = (f" WHERE {_config['date_column']} >='{_config['date_column']}' and "
                     f"{_config['date_column']} < '{_config['date_column']}'")
    QUERY = (f"SELECT {_config['selectcolumnslist']} FROM {_config['source_db']}.{_config['source_schema']}."
             f"{_config['source_table']}")
```

Let's see how above loop is working
In the loop we are creating the where condition using the date list,
the where condition looks like below.

When the loop will run for the first time the WHERE condition
will look like below
WHERE lastmodifieddate >=' 2023-01-01 00:00:00' and
lastmodifieddate <'2023-01-02 00:00:00'
You can see here we are fetching one days data i.e. of 1st January.

In the next iteration of the loop the where condition will look like
below
WHERE lastmodifieddate >=' 2023-01-02 00:00:00' and
lastmodifieddate <'2023-01-03 00:00:00'

i.e. in the next iteration we will fetch data of 2nd Jan. Likewise in
the loop we will fetch the entire table day wise.

In the last iteration when the if(date_count == len(date_list) – 1)
becomes True, the where condition will be as below
WHERE lastmodifieddate >=' 2025-01-05 00:00:00'
This will ensure that in the last iteration all records fetched up to
the current time.

We are done with how to fetch the data.

Lets see how we insert data into different types of databases.

Insert data into the target

First take case of Bigquery
There are two ways to insert data into Bigquery

- Insert_rows_from_dataframe
  Method: Part of the google.cloud.bigquery.Client.
  How it works
  Sends rows to BigQuery one at a time (or in small batches) using the streaming insert API.

  Data is added directly to the table without requiring intermediate storage.

- load_table_from_dataframe
  Method: Part of the google.cloud.bigquery.Client.
  How it works:
  Uses a bulk-loading process by uploading the

  DataFrame as a file to temporary storage and then loading it into BigQuery.

  Supports high-throughput operations.

load_table_from_dataframe function can sometimes cause Quota exceeded error so using **insert_rows_from_dataframe** is preferred

Python Code

```
table                                    =                        dest_con.get_table("{}.{}.
{}".format(_config["destination_db"],_config["destination_schema"],_config["destination_table"]))
dest_con.insert_rows_from_dataframe(table,dataframe)
```

Lets now write reusable data processiong function to sync legacy data

◆ ◆ ◆

We may have requirement to insert data into other databases apart from BigQuery

Let's proceed to insert data in other databases:(MySQL, MSSql,Postgres)

When we fetch data from source we get a pandas data frame.
Using Pandas **to_sql** method as below we insert data into the target tables

Python Code

```
_df.to_sql(_config["destination_table"],dest_con, schema=_config["destination_schema"],
        if_exists='append', index=False, chunksize=10000, method="multi")
```

to_sql will insert data into target table and as mentioned above in the **chunksize** parameter in a batch of 10000 records

With this we have completed a full data sync scenario.
In the next page, let's discuss regular sync.

◆ ◆ ◆

Incremental sync: Fetch data from source incrementally.

Once full sync is done then we need to regularly sync data from live source to data warehouse.

As discussed earlier while doing regular sync operations we have to sync incrementally.

Incremental means when a sync operation finishes then the next sync should start from the time where the previous sync was completed.

This timestamp has to be from the source table and not the system time.

To do incrementally we have to note down the timestamp during each sync operation and start from the noted timestamp during the next sync operation.

Let's define one variable as **max_date_last_sync**.
This variable will keep track of the timestamp of the sync operation.

While doing sync we do fetch operations in chunks.

For each chunk we note down the max last modified date of that chunk and store it in a list.

Once sync operation is finished we find the max last modified date from the list.

In this way we get the timestamp upto which the data was synced.

During the next sync operation we start from the max timestamp we found from the list.

Sometimes it may happen that in the source the records may get added slightly late after the previous sync was complete.

When this happens the delayed records are missed from the next sync

Let's see how.
Assume **max_date_last_sync="2025-01-05 12:30:13"**
This means in the previous sync the records were synced upto **"2025-01-05 12:30:13"**.

Suppose after the previous sync completed then some records got updated or added with timestamp **"2025-01-05 12:29:13"**

As the next sync will start from **max_date_last_sync>="2025-01-05 12:30:13"**

The newly added records with timestamp "2025-01-05 12:29:13" will be missed and will not be syned to the target table

To ensure that the records are not missed, we should subtract 10 minutes from the **max_date_last_sync** so that there is some overlap between previous sync and current sync.

Whether we should subtract 10 minutes or more or less can be judged by the experience there is no specific rule to this.

Towards the end of the book we will see what fallback we can add for this.

Lets enhance our reusable framewrok by writing reusable function for incremental data processing.

Python Code

```
def sync_data():
    max_date_last_sync ="2025-01-05 12: 30:13"
    QUERY = "SELECT id, name, salary from employee"
    datetime_obj = datetime.strptime(max_date_last_sync,  format "%Y-%m-%d %H:%M:%S")
    # Subtract 10 minutes using timedelta
    new_datetime_obj = datetime_obj - timedelta(minutes=10)
    # Convert the datetime object back to a string
    max_date_last_sync_minus10 = new_datetime_obj.strftime("%Y-%m-%d %H:%M: %S")
    condition = f" WHERE {_config['src_date_column']} >='{max_date_last_sync_minus10}'"
    list_max_date = [] # list to hold max date of each chunk
    src_con    # initialize soruce connection
    dest_con # initialize destination connection

    QUERY = QUERY + condition
    chunk = pd.read_sql(QUERY, con=src_con, chunksize=10000) # read data in chunks
    for records_df in chunk:
        max_date = records_df[_config['src_date_column']].max()
        list_max_date.append(max_date)
        records_df.to_sql(paramter list....) #insert / update operation for PG,Mysql,MSSQL
        table = dest_con.get_table("{}.{}.{}".format( *args _config["destination_db"], _config["destination_schema"],
                                        _config["destination_table"]))
        dest_con.insert_rows_from_dataframe(table, records_df) #insert / update operation for BigQuery
        ## after the loop is complete we get a list of max lastmodifieddate of the  ## source,
        ## from that list again we need find max date
    max_date_df = pd.DataFrame(list_max_date)
    max date last sync = max date df.max()
```

The benefit of this approach is that even if the sync failed multiple times, it will always start from the recorded max_date_last_sync of the last successful sync,ensuring no data loss.

There is an alternative for incremental sync in which we do not have to maintain the max_date_last_sync.

In the alternate approach we do not have max_date_last_sync noted from the previous sync.

Here we use INTERVAL in the WHERE condition,

for example WHERE lastmodifieddate >= NOW() - INTERVAL 30 minutes

In this approach also we put overlapping intervals.

For example if the sync is running every 10 minutes then we put interval as 20 minutes.

Now lets consider one scenario.

Suppose if the jobs failed at 10am, 10.10am , 10.20am, 10.30am, 10.40am and succeeded at 10.50am, that means that it was not synced for 50 minutes.

At 10.50 the where condition will look like
WHERE lastmodifieddate >= NOW() - INTERVAL 20 minutes.

So data will get synced from 10.30am onwards.

This will result in data loss as the sync failed from 10 am and at 10 am it would have started from 9.40 am.

To handle this scenario we maintain failure_count, by default it is set to 1.
failure_count = 1

When the jobs fails we increment the count by 1

Then we convert the failure count to minutes

failure_count_to_minutes = str(int(failure_count) * 10)

we multiplied by 10 because our sync interval is 10 minutes.

To create overlapping condition we should add 20 to it.

failure_count_to_minutes = failure_count_to_minutes + 20

condition = f" WHERE lastmodifieddate >= NOW() - INTERVAL '{failure_count_to_minutes} minutes'"

Lets dry run our logic with the failure scenario.

As the sync failed between 10am to 10.40am the failure count

would be 5

failure_count_to_minutes will be 50 and we will add 20 to it to create overlapping condition

The where condition will automatically become to

condition = f" WHERE lastmodifieddate >= NOW() - INTERVAL 70 minutes "

So our common framework is now programmed to cover failure scenarios

We have now understood Full sync and incremental sync.

Recap

- *So far we have understood how to make connections.*

- *Define data pipeline.*

- *How to do full sync.*

- *How to fetch data in chunks.*

- *How to fetch incremental data.*

- *Handle failure scenarios to avoid data loss.*

Remaining part now is the insertion into the target.

In the next page onwards Let's explore insertion scenarios.

Let's proceed to the scenarios below.

1.   Fetch data from source at regular interval and Insert new   records and update existing records in the target called as Upsert operation. Suppose we fetch data from source in a chunk of 10k records. The chunk will have new records as well as existing modified records.

2.   Fetch data from source at regular interval and Insert only - only insert records into the target no update operation here.

3.   Fetch data from source at regular interval and Delete the existing records of the target and insert new records, for example if certain report requires only daily sales data.

Let's cover 2,3 first as they are almost similar.

Scenario 2,3 comes under regular incremental sync with insert only operation and Delete and Insert operation.

The scenario 2 comes into picture when in the source only new records are added and existing records are not modified.

In this case we only need to perform insert operation in the target

Scenario 3 comes into picture when in the source everyday new data is generated as part of some business logic and old data must be removed.

So we delete the records from the target and insert new records from the source.

Let's see on the next page how we handle this in the code.

Scenario 2, we perform insert operation no updates in target

Our data fetch logic remains the same for scenario 2,3 as discussed above for incremental sync. Either we will use **max_date_last_sync approach** or **failure_count** approach to get incremental data.

```python
condition = f" WHERE {_config['src_date_column']} >='{max_date_last_sync_minus10}'"
list_max_date = [] #list to hold max date of each chunk
src_con  # initialize soruce connection
dest_con  # initialize destination connection
QUERY = QUERY + condition
chunk = pd.read_sql(QUERY, con=src_con, chunksize=10000) # read data in chunks
for records_df in chunk:
    max_date = records_df[_config['src_date_column']].max()
    list_max_date.append(max_date)
    records_df.to_sql(_config["destination_table"], dest_con, schema=_config["destination_schema"],
    if_exists='append', index=False, chunksize=10000, method="multi") # for MySQL,PG,MsSQL
    table = dest_con.get_table("{}.{}.{}".format( *args: _config["destination_db"], _config["destination_schema"],
                                    _config["destination_table"]))
    dest_con.insert_rows_from_dataframe(table, records_df) #insert / update operation for BigQuery
```

method="multi" parameter in the to_sql ensures that we are doing only insert operation

Next lets see delete and insert operation

Scenario 3, delete the target data and insert new data from source

Data fetch and insert logic is same as above, only change is we deleted the records before inserting.

The python code will look as below

```
condition = f" WHERE {_config['src_date_column']} >='{max_date_last_sync_minus10}'"
list_max_date = []   # list to hold max date of each chunk
src_con   # initialize soruce connection
dest_con   # initialize destination connection
QUERY = QUERY + condition
del_query = f"DELETE FROM {_config["destination_schema"]}.{_config['destination_table']} WHERE 1=1"
dest_con.execute(del_query)
chunk = pd.read_sql(QUERY, con=src_con, chunksize=10000)   # read data in chunks
for records_df in chunk:
    max_date = records_df[_config['src_date_column']].max()
    list_max_date.append(max_date)
    records_df.to_sql(_config["destination_table"], dest_con, schema=_config["destination_schema"],
    if_exists='append', index=False, chunksize=10000, method="multi")   # for MySQL,PG,MsSQL
    table = dest_con.get_table("{}.{}.{}".format( *args: _config["destination_db"], _config["destination_schema"],
                                                  _config["destination_table"]))
    dest_con.insert_rows_from_dataframe(table, records_df) #insert / update operation for BigQuery
```

In this Scenario 3, the change we did is to add delete query before the data fetch loop and the insert logic remains the same

In the next section lets see upsert operation.

In the upsert operation the logic to fetch the data from the source remains the same only change comes in the to_sql mehtod of pandas

First we define a function to perform upsert operation.
Then call the same function from the to_sql method of pandas in the method parameter

```
records_df.to_sql((_config["destination_table"],          dest_con,
schema=_config["destination_schema"],
                              if_exists='append', index=False, chunksize=10000,
method=upsert_func)
```

Lets enhance our common framework by defining upsert function for mssql, mysql,postgres, Bigquery Dbs

On the next page Lets start with MSSQL

M ssql Upsert function
Doing upsert in mssql requires a temporay table.

Remember we have "destination_table_stg" in _config dictionary we are going to use below keys of the _config dictionary

destination_keys
insertcolumnslist
on_duplicate
destination_table
destination_table_stg

In the _config dictionary we mention
"destination_table_stg": "#temp"

and we perform insert only operation in the #temp table using pandas to_sql

This way we get data inserted in temporary table.

Then using MERGE query we merge from temporary table to main table.

Our fully functional, fully automated mssql upsert function will look like bleow

```
def mssql_upsert(conn):
    on_condition = ""
    insert_values = ""
    update_Values = ""
    for items in _config["destination_keys"].split(","):
        if (len(items) > 0):
            on_condition = on_condition + "Source." + items + "=" + "Target." + items + " and "
    on_condition = on_condition[:len(on_condition) - 4]

    for items in _config["insertcolumnslist"].split(","):
        insert_values = insert_values + "Source." + items + ","
    insert_values = insert_values.rstrip(",")

    for items in _config["on_duplicate"].split(","):
        update_Values = update_Values + "Target." + items + "=" + "Source." + items + ","

    update_Values = update_Values.rstrip(",")
    update_Values = update_Values + ";"

    merge_query = (f"MERGE {_config['destination_table']} AS Target USING {_config['destination_table_stg']} "
                   f"AS Source ON {on_condition} WHEN NOT MATCHED BY Target THEN INSERT ("
                   f"{_config['insertcolumnslist']}) VALUES ({insert_values} ) WHEN MATCHED THEN UPDATE SET  "
                   f"{update_Values}")
    print("@@@@@@@@@ merge_query ", merge_query)
    conn.execute(merge_query)
```

We will call mssql_upsert function after the for loop block
for records_df in chunk:

P ostgres upsert function would look like below

```
def postgres_upsert(table, conn, keys, data_iter):
    # print("In postgres_upsert")
    metadata = MetaData(schema=_config["destination_schema"])
    # print("metadata: {}".format(metadata))
    metadata.bind = conn
    table = Table( *args: _config["destination_table"], metadata,
    # get list of fields making up primary key
    # print("table: {}".format(table))
    primary_keys = [key.name for key in inspect(table).primary_key]
    # print("primary_keys {}".format(primary_keys))
    data = [dict(zip(keys, row)) for row in data_iter]
    # print("@@@@@@@@ data", data)
    # print("table.table: {}".format(table))
    insert_statement = insert(table).values(data)
    # print("insert_statement: {}".format(insert_statement))
    ss = {c.key: c for c in insert_statement.excluded}
    key_set = {}
    columns_to_sync = _config["insertcolumnslist"].split(
        ",")
    for column_name in columns_to_sync:
        key_set[column_name] = ss[column_name]
    upsert_statement = insert_statement.on_conflict_do_update(
        index_elements=primary_keys,
        set_=key_set,
    )
    # print("@@@@@@@@@@@@@@ upsert_statement ", upsert_statement)
    conn.execute(upsert_statement)
```

◆ ◆ ◆

Mysql Upsert function, for mysql upsert we use ON DUPLICATE KEY update SQL synctax this will insert records and if duplicate primary key is found then update.

```python
def mysql_upsert(table, conn, keys, data_iter):
    data1 = [dict(zip(keys, row)) for row in data_iter]
    insert_columnslist = str(_config["insertcolumnslist"]).split(",")
    subquery = ""
    count = 0
    for rows in data1:
        partquery = ""
        count = count + 1
        for columns in insert_columnslist:  # <<2>>
            if (str(type(rows[columns])).find("datetime") > 0):
                rows[columns] = str(rows[columns]).split(".")[0]
                partquery = partquery + "'" + str(rows[columns]) + "',"
                continue
            if (rows[columns] is None):
                rows[columns] = 'NULL'
            if (type(rows[columns]) is str):
                partquery = partquery + "'" + replaceSpchr(str(rows[columns])) + "',"
            else:
                partquery = partquery + str(rows[columns]) + ","
        partquery = partquery.replace(_old="'NULL'", _new="NULL")
        partquery = partquery.rstrip(",")
        partquery = " (" + partquery + "),"
        subquery = subquery + partquery
    on_duplicate = ""
    if (len(_config["on_duplicate"]) > 0):
        columns_to_update = str(_config["on_duplicate"]).split(",")
        for names in columns_to_update:
            on_duplicate = on_duplicate + _config[
                "destination_table"] + "." + names + " = VALUES(" + names + "),"
        on_duplicate = " ON DUPLICATE KEY update  " + on_duplicate

    query = "INSERT INTO " + _config["destination_db"] + "." + _config[
        "destination_table"] + " (" + _config["insertcolumnslist"] + ") values " + subquery.rstrip(
        ",") + on_duplicate.rstrip(",")
    try:
        conn.execute(query)
    except BaseException as e:
        traceback.print_exc()
```

The way to call this function is as below
Inside the for loop we call this funcion in the to_sql method paramter

query_job_df.to_sql(_config["destination_table"],dest_con, schema=_config["destination_schema"], if_exists='append', index=False, chunksize=1000, method=mysql_upsert)

Bigquery Upsert function

Doing upsert in Bigquery requires a temporay table.

We have "destination_table_stg" in _config dictionary

In the _config dictionary we mention the name of the stageing table

"destination_table_stg": "<<maintable_stage"

and we perform insert only operation in the stage table using **insert_rows_from_dataframe(table,dataframe)**

This way we get data inserted in temporary table.

Then using MERGE query we merge from temporary table to main table.

Our fully functional, fully automated Bigquery upsert function will look like below

```
def bigquery_upsert():
    on_condition = ""
    update_vals = ""
    for items in _config["upsert_keys"].split(","):
        on_condition = on_condition + "T." + items + "=" + "S." + items + " and "
    on_condition = on_condition.rstrip(" and ")

    for items in _config["insertcolumnslist"].split(","):
        update_vals = update_vals + "T." + items + "=" + "S." + items

    update_vals = update_vals[:-1]
    merge_query = (f"MERGE {_config['destination_table']} T USING {_config['destination_staging_table']} "
        f"S ON ( {on_condition} ) WHEN MATCHED THEN UPDATE SET {update_vals} WHEN NOT MATCHED BY "
        f"TARGET THEN INSERT ({_config['insertcolumnslist']} ) VALUES ({_config['insertcolumnslist']}) ")
```

We will call bigquery_upsert function after the end of for loop block

        for records_df in chunk:

All the above upsert functions are arrived at continous efforts of over 2 years by adjusting different scenarios i faced over the years of running data pipelines

A quick wrapup of what we learnt so far

- So far we have understood how to make connection.

- How to do full sync.

- How to fetch data in chunk.

- How to fetch incremental data.

- Handle failure scenarios to avoid data loss.

- How to do incremental insert only operation.

- How to do incremental delete and insert operation.

- How to do incremental upsert operation

Sometimes we have to do upsert operation in Full sync also as there is a possibilty of having duplciate records.

With above knowledge we are now in a position to build ETL Data Pipeline.

Once we build a pipeline we must deploy it somewhere so that it is executed.

We should be able to schedule the pipeline

We should get notifed of the failures in exuecution

We should have the option to retry after failure.

We should be able to get a dashboard of pipelines.

All these features we get out of the box in Apache Airflow.

In the next section we will get inroduced to Apache Airflow

7. INTRODUCTION TO APACHE AIRFLOW

Apache Airflow is a robust, scalable, and flexible platform for orchestrating complex workflows or pipelines. Developed initially by Airbnb in 2014 and later open-sourced under the Apache Software Foundation, it has become one of the most popular tools for workflow automation in data engineering and machine learning. It provides a way to programmatically author, schedule, and monitor workflows, ensuring reliable execution of tasks in the right order.

What is Apache Airflow?

At its core, Apache Airflow is a **workflow orchestration tool**. It allows users to define workflows as Directed Acyclic Graphs (DAGs) using Python code. These DAGs represent the sequence in which tasks should be executed and how they are interdependent. Airflow's primary goal is to ensure workflows are executed in the correct order, even in dynamic and distributed environments.

Airflow's key functionalities include:

1. **Authoring Workflows**: Workflows are defined using Python scripts, making them flexible and easy to version control.

2. **Scheduling**: Airflow ensures that workflows are triggered at specific times or intervals.

3. **Monitoring**: A built-in web interface allows users to monitor running workflows, troubleshoot failures, and view logs.

Key Components of Apache Airflow

Airflow has several essential components that work together to manage workflows efficiently:

1. **DAG (Directed Acyclic Graph):** A DAG is the fundamental building block of Airflow. It represents a

collection of tasks that need to be executed in a specific order. Each task in a DAG is represented as a node, while the edges represent dependencies between tasks.

2. **Task:** A task is a single unit of work, such as running a Python script, querying a database, or triggering an API. Tasks can have dependencies, ensuring they are executed in the right sequence.

3. **Scheduler:** The scheduler is responsible for triggering tasks based on the defined schedule. It determines when to start each task and ensures that task dependencies are met.

4. **Executor:** The executor handles the actual execution of tasks. Airflow supports multiple executors, such as **LocalExecutor** (for small-scale deployments) and **CeleryExecutor** (for distributed environments).

5. **Web Server:** Airflow provides a user-friendly web interface to monitor DAGs, inspect logs, view task progress, and manage workflows. The web server makes it easy for users to interact with the system.

6. **Metadata Database:** Airflow stores metadata about DAGs, task states, logs, and other configuration settings in a database. Supported databases include PostgreSQL and MySQL.

Key Features of Apache Airflow

1. **Dynamic Workflow Authoring:** Unlike static configuration files, Airflow uses Python code to define workflows. This allows users to write dynamic workflows that can adapt based on parameters, conditions, or external inputs.

2. **Modular Design:** Airflow's modular architecture makes it easy to extend and customize. Plugins can be added to integrate Airflow with external systems or introduce new operators.

3. **Extensive Operator Library:** Airflow includes a wide variety of pre-built operators, such as BashOperator, PythonOperator, and MySqlOperator, as well as hooks

for connecting to external services like AWS, Google Cloud, and Apache Hive.

4. **Scalability:** Airflow can scale from running simple workflows on a single machine to managing complex pipelines across a distributed cluster using CeleryExecutor or KubernetesExecutor.

5. **Monitoring and Alerting:** Airflow provides detailed logs for every task, making it easier to debug workflows. Users can also set up alerts to notify them of task failures or delays.

6. **Integration with External Tools:** Airflow seamlessly integrates with a wide range of tools, such as cloud providers (AWS, GCP, Azure), databases, big data frameworks (Hadoop, Spark), and machine learning platforms.

Common Use Cases for Apache Airflow

1. **Data Pipelines:** Airflow is widely used to orchestrate ETL (Extract, Transform, Load) workflows, ensuring data is ingested, transformed, and loaded into target systems on a regular schedule.

2. **Machine Learning Workflows:** Machine learning teams use Airflow to manage training pipelines, hyperparameter tuning, and deployment processes.

3. **DevOps and Automation:** Airflow automates repetitive DevOps tasks, such as database backups, log rotations, and infrastructure provisioning.

4. **Cloud Data Orchestration:** Airflow integrates with cloud services like AWS Glue, Google BigQuery, and Azure Data Factory, making it a valuable tool for cloud-native data workflows.

5.

Advantages of Apache Airflow

1. **Open Source:** Airflow is free and open-source, backed by a large community of developers who contribute regularly to its improvement.

2. **Flexibility:** With Python as the language for defining workflows, users can leverage the full power of a programming language to build complex, dynamic pipelines.

3. **Visibility:** The web UI provides real-time visibility into task statuses, execution timelines, and logs, making it easy to manage workflows.

4. **Extensibility:** Users can create custom operators, sensors, and hooks to extend Airflow's functionality to suit their specific needs.

5. **Community and Ecosystem:** The large and active Airflow community provides a wealth of resources, plugins, and integrations.

Challenges and Limitations

1. **Steep Learning Curve:** While powerful, Airflow can be complex for beginners to learn and configure, especially for distributed deployments.

2. **Not Ideal for Real-Time Processing:** Airflow is designed for batch processing and is not well-suited for real-time, low-latency workflows.

3. **Resource-Intensive:** The scheduler and web server can become resource-intensive in large-scale environments, requiring careful optimization.

4. **Limited Task Retries:** While Airflow allows task retries, handling transient failures requires custom logic in some cases.

Conclusion

Apache Airflow is a powerful tool for orchestrating workflows in modern data engineering and machine learning pipelines. Its flexibility, scalability, and integration capabilities make it a go-to solution for organizations managing complex workflows. While it has its challenges, with the right configuration and understanding, Airflow can significantly enhance workflow automation and monitoring. As the ecosystem evolves, Apache Airflow continues to set the standard for open-source workflow orchestration.

8. WRITING OUR FIRST REAL DATA PIPELINE

Quick wrap up

- So far we have understood how to make connection.

- How to do full sync.

- How to fetch data in chunk.

- How to fetch incremental data.

- Handle failure scenarios to avoid data loss.

- How to do incremental insert only operation.

- How to do incremental delete and insert operation.

- How to do incremental upsert operation
- Using apache airflow
- Handle failures, retry,scheduling

We will merge all that we understood so fat and write our first real data pipeline and host it on apache airflow.

Lets define our problem

Application data is being stored in postgres table.
We have datalake in bigquery.
Analytics team wants the data from postgres to datalake.

Lets break down the problem into smaller task.

As it is the first time we are moving the postgres table to datalake that means we need to first sync legacy data right from the first record to the latest records and then start incremental sync.

This requires us to find from which date we need to sync the data, so we must know how to find the first record of the table.

We know first record by some date column or auto incremented ID column

Step 1. We must check if there is some column which will help us move data from PG to BQ in incremental fashion, column like lastmodifieddate, autoincremented ID column

Step 2. Get the the minimum lastmodified date of the table.This date will be our starting point to sync the data.

Step 3. Check if the column names of source and destination are   exactly same, if not then need to define column mapping in _config dictionary in **src_dest_mapping**

Step 4. Write the DAG (Airflow task is called a DAG) and deploy.

Let's create tables for our experiment in PG and BQ

Create table in Postgres

```
CREATE TABLE employee (
    employee_id SERIAL PRIMARY KEY,
    first_name VARCHAR(50),
    last_name VARCHAR(50),
    hire_date DATE,
    salary NUMERIC(10, 2),
    is_active BOOLEAN
);
```

Equivalent table in Bigquery

```
CREATE TABLE `your_project.your_dataset.employee` (
    employee_id INT64 NOT NULL,
    first_name STRING,
    last_name STRING,
    date_of_hire DATE,
```

salary NUMERIC,
is_active BOOL,
last_workingdate DATE ## this column is not present in source table
);

INSERT INTO employee (first_name, last_name, hire_date, salary, is_active)

SELECT

'FirstName' || generate_series(1, 1000),

'LastName' || generate_series(1, 1000),

CURRENT_DATE - (random() * 3650)::int,

(random() * 10)::numeric(10, 2),

(random() > 0.5)::boolean

FROM generate_series(1, 10000);

we have changed hire_date in source to date_of_hire in destination to understand how source and destination mapping works

In this table we have hire_date as a column which we can use to do legacy sync as well as incremental sync.

So let's get started with writing our first ETL data pipeline.

Let's define the structure of the ETL Job.

Naming convention for ETL jobs file should be such that the name itself explains the job.

a sample name would look like ETL_<<srcdb>><<*srctable*>>_<<destdb>>_<<desttable>>.py

Accordingly we will name our first ETL job as

ETL_PG_airflowdata_employee_BQ_airflowdata_employee.py

The python file will be divided in below sections.

<< necessary imports>>

<< define data pipeline>>

<<date range generator for legacy sync>>

<<read and load function>>

<<Airflow DAG definition>>

```python
## below import for airflow dag definition
from airflow import DAG
from airflow.operators.python_operator import PythonOperator
## for making connection
from sqlalchemy import create_engine
## for data processing
import pandas as pd
## for bigquery operations
from google.cloud import bigquery
## for debugging error
import traceback
##miscellaneous
from datetime import datetime, timedelta
import pendulum
import os

## import credentials files global.py which will have dictionary for
## storing credentials like
creds={"localhost_username": "airflow","localhost_password": "airflow"}
from globals import creds

## airflow by default takes UTC as timezone, so let's define our local
## timezone
local_tz = pendulum.timezone("Asia/Kolkata")

## lets define our _config dictionary which will define our data pipeline
_config = {
    "metadata": "This job is request by analytics team for their ",
```

```python
_config = {
    "metadata": "This job is request by analytics team for their ",
    "gcp_key": "~/airflow/ServiceAccount.json",
    "schedule": None,   ## for legacy sync we will keep it manual sync later we will schedule it
    "dag_id": "ETL_PG_airflowdata_employee_BQ_airflowdata_employee",
    "source_driver": "postgresql",
    "source_host": "localhost",
    "source_port": "5432",
    "source_username": creds["localhost_username"],
    "source_password": creds["localhost_password"],
    "source_db": "airflow_data",
    "source_schema": "public",
    "source_table": "employee",
    "source_date_column": "hire_date",
    "selectcolumnslist":"employee_id, first_name, last_name, hire_date, salary, is_active",
    "selectcondition": "",
    "destination_driver": "bigquery",
    "destination_host": "",   ## not required for bigquery
    "destination_port": "",   ## not required for bigquery
    "destination_schema_stg": "",   ## we need this for incremental sync, skip for now
    "destination_table_stg": "",## we need this for incremental sync, skip for now
    "destination_db": "datalake",
    "destination_schema": "airflow_data",
    "destination_table": "employee",
    "destination_username": "",   ## not required for bigquery
    "destination_password": "",## not required for bigquery
    "destination_password": "",## not required for bigquery
    "destination_keys": "",   ## need to incremental sync, to insert and merge
    "insertcolumnslist":"employee_id,first_name,last_name,date_of_hire,salary,is_active",
    "on_duplicate":"employee_id,first_name,last_name,date_of_hire,salary,is_active",
    "src_dest_mapping": {"hire_date":"date_of_hire"},
    "fillnull": "",## not required in this job
    "new_columns": {"last_workingdate":None},   ## as this column is not in src we will
                                                ##add and assign default as NULL value
    "default_values": "",## not required in this job
}

##bigquery credentials files
os.environ["GOOGLE_APPLICATION_CREDENTIALS"] = _config["gcp_key"]
##connection function
def get_connection(driver, connflag):
    connection_str = ""
    if (connflag == "src"):
        connection_str = (f"{_config['source_username']}:quote({_config['source_password']})@"
                f"{_config['source_host']}:{_config['source_port']}/{_config["source_db"]}")
    elif (connflag == "dest"):
        connection_str = (f"{_config['destination_username']}:quote({_config['destination_password']})@"
                f"{_config['destination_host']}:{_config['destination_port']}/{_config["destination_db"]}")
    if (driver == "mysql"):
        engine = create_engine("mysql://" +
        connection_str,isolation_level='AUTOCOMMIT')
    elif (driver == "postgresql"):
        engine = create_engine("postgresql://" + connection_str)
```

```python
    elif (driver == "postgresql"):
        engine = create_engine("postgresql://" + connection_str)
    elif (driver == "mssql"):
        engine = create_engine("mssql+pymssql://" +
      connection_str,isolation_level='AUTOCOMMIT')
    elif (driver == "bigquery"):
        if(connflag=="src"):
            engine = create_engine( url: 'bigquery://',
          credentials_path=_config["gcp_key"])
        else:
            client = bigquery.Client()
            return client
    if (connflag == "src"):
        conn = engine.connect().execution_options(stream_results=True)
    else:
        conn = engine.connect().execution_options()
    return conn


## below functions returns day wise date list from the minimum hire_date ## to the current date
def date_time_list(start_date,end_date):
    step = timedelta(days=1)
    result = []
    while start_date < end_date:
        result.append(start_date.strftime('%Y-%m-%d %H:%M:%S'))
        start_date += step
    return result
## this is our main function where all sync activity will be done
def loadrecords():
    try:
        print("@@@@@@@@@@ Hi Job Started")
        start_date = datetime( year: 2015,  month: 1,  day: 16,  hour: 00,  minute: 00,  second: 00)
        end_date = datetime( year: 2024,  month: 1,  day: 15,  hour: 23,  minute: 59,  second: 59)
        date_list = date_time_list(start_date, end_date)
        src_driver = _config["source_driver"]
        dest_driver = _config["destination_driver"]
        src_con = get_connection(_config["source_driver"], connflag: "src")
        print("@@@@@@@@@@ connection create to" + src_driver)

        dest_con = get_connection(_config["destination_driver"], connflag: "dest")
        print("@@@@@@@@@@ connection create to" + dest_driver)
        for date_count in range(len(date_list)):
            if (date_count == len(date_list)):
                condition = f"WHERE {_config['src_date_column']}>='{date_list[date_count - 1]}"
            else:
                condition = (f"WHERE {_config['src_date_column']} >= '{date_list[date_count]}' and "
                            f"{_config['src_date_column']} < '{date_list[date_count + 1]} '")
            QUERY = (f"SELECT {_config['selectcolumnslist']} FROM {_config['source_db']}."
                    f"{_config['source_table']} {condition}")
            print("@@@@@@@@@@ QUERY " + QUERY)
            count = 0
            chunk = pd.read_sql(QUERY, con=src_con, chunksize=100000)

            for query_job_df in chunk:
```

```
        for query_job_df in chunk:
            count = count + len(query_job_df)
            if (len(_config["src_dest_mapping"]) > 0):
                query_job_df.rename(columns=_config["src_dest_mapping"],
                inplace=True)
            loc = 7 ## we want the new column to be add after 6th position
            for key, values in _config["new_columns"].items():
                query_job_df.insert(loc, key, values)
                loc = loc + 1
            table = dest_con.get_table("{}.{}.{}".format( *args: _config["destination_db"],
                                    _config["destination_schema"],
                                    _config["destination_table"]))
            dest_con.insert_rows_from_dataframe(table, query_job_df)
            print(f"@@@@@@@@@@ record count={count} for date {date_list[date_count]}")
    except BaseException as e:
        traceback.print_exc()
        print("@@@@@@@@@@ scheduler completed with error ")
        exit()
    finally:
        print("@@@@@@@@@@ scheduler completed")


default_args = {'owner': 'airflow',
                'start_date': datetime( year: 2025,  month: 1,  day: 8, tzinfo=local_tz),
                }


default_args = {'owner': 'airflow',
                'start_date': datetime( year: 2025,  month: 1,  day: 8, tzinfo=local_tz),
                }
dag = DAG(_config["dag_id"], schedule_interval=_config["schedule"], default_args=default_args,
            catchup=False)
with dag:
    loadrecords = PythonOperator(task_id="task_id_loadrecords", python_callable=loadrecords)


loadrecords
```

9. DEPLOYMENT ON APACHE AIRFLOW

Our first airflow DAG is ready, now we need to deploy and execute.

Let understand the Airflow directory structure

AIRFLOW_HOME

—-------------logs

—-------------dags

—-------------plugins

The airflow tasks need to be copied to dags directory.

The Airflow scheduler scans the dag directory for new files.

The new files are compiled and deployed by the scheduler.

By default the airflow DAGS are paused, so we need to enable it.

Once we enable the DAGS start to execute as per the scheduled time.

We have completed one time full sync of the requested table, lets now try and schedule a regular job to sync data in near real time.

Airflow supports a minimum scheduling frequency of 1 minute.

Let's proceed. Most of the code that we wrote for full sync will utilized with some changes to handle every minute incremental sync

Lets understand the changes we need for this every minute job.

We need to do incremental sync, means we need to start from where we finished the previous sync.

As it is incremental it possible that some records will be new and others may be existing records but got modified.

So in Bigquery terminology we need to merge the changes in to the target BQ table. So that the new records are inserted while existing records are updated.

For merging we need a staging table.

We insert incremental data into staging table and from staging table we merge into the main target table.

So this merging activity takes care of new records, updates to existing records, and deleted records. Deletion is basically an update operation as the production records are soft deleted with some deleted flag being made true.

> *If there are hard deleted records then we have to truncate the target table and do full sync.For bigger tables we can't full sync frequently so it is better to have soft delete and schedule maintenance activity monthly to hard delete the soft deleted records from source and target.Or other option is to use CDC based data sync.*

ETL_PG_airflowdata_employee_BQ_airflowdata_employee.py

<< necessary imports>>

<< define data pipeline>>

<<date range generator for legacy sync>>

<<read and load function>>

<<Airflow DAG definition>>

below import for airflow dag definition

```
from airflow import DAG
from airflow.operators.python_operator import PythonOperator
```

```
## below import for airflow dag definition
from airflow import DAG
from airflow.operators.python_operator import PythonOperator
## for making connection
from sqlalchemy import create_engine
## for data processing
import pandas as pd
## for bigquery operations
from google.cloud import bigquery
## for debugging error
import traceback
##miscellaneous
from datetime import datetime, timedelta
import pendulum
import os
## import credentials files global.py which will have dictionary for  storing credentials like
## creds={"localhost_username": "airflow","localhost_password": "airflow"}
from globals import creds

## airflow by default takes UTC as timezone, so let's define our local
## timezone
local_tz = pendulum.timezone("Asia/Kolkata")

## lets define our _config dictionary which will define our data pipeline
_config = {
    "metadata": "This job is request by analytics team for their ",
    "gcp_key": "~/airflow/ServiceAccount.json",
```

```python
"schedule": None,  ## for legacy sync we will keep it manual sync later we will
## schedule it
"dag_id": "ETL_PG_airflowdata_employee_BQ_airflowdata_employee",
"source_driver": "postgresql",
"source_host": "localhost",
"source_port": "5432",
"source_username": creds["localhost_username"],
"source_password": creds["localhost_password"],
"source_db": "airflow_data",
"source_schema": "public",
"source_table": "employee",
"source_date_column": "hire_date",
"selectcolumnslist":"employee_id, first_name, last_name, hire_date, salary, is_active",
"selectcondition": "",
"destination_driver": "bigquery",
 "destination_host": "",  ## not required for bigquery
"destination_port": "",  ## not required for bigquery
"destination_db": "datalake",
"destination_schema": "airflow_data",
"destination_table": "employee",
"destination_table_stg": "employee_stg", ## stage table for merge activity
"destination_username": "",  ## not required for bigquery
"destination_password": "",  ## not required for bigquery
"destination_keys": "employee_id",
"insertcolumnslist": "employee_id,first_name,last_name,date_of_hire,salary,is_active",
"on_duplicate":"employee_id,first_name,last_name,date_of_hire,salary,is_active",
"src_dest_mapping": {"hire_date":"date_of_hire"},
```

```python
        "src_dest_mapping": {"hire_date":"date_of_hire"},
        "fillnull": "",  ## not required in this job
        "new_columns": {"last_workingdate":None},  ## as this column is not in src we will
        ##add and assign default as NULL value
        "default_values": "",  ## not required in this job
    }
    # bigquery credentials files
    os.environ["GOOGLE_APPLICATION_CREDENTIALS"] = _config["gcp_key"]
    #Bigquery merge function
    def bigquery_upsert(dest_con):  1 usage
        on_condition = ""
        update_vals = ""
        for items in _config["upsert_keys"].split(","):
            on_condition = on_condition + "T." + items + "=" + "S." + items + " and "
        on_condition = on_condition.rstrip(" and ")

        for items in _config["insertcolumnslist"].split(","):
            update_vals = update_vals + "T." + items + "=" + "S." + items

        update_vals = update_vals[:-1]
        merge_query = (f"MERGE {_config['destination_table']} T USING {_config['destination_table_stg']} "
            f"S ON ( {on_condition} ) WHEN MATCHED THEN UPDATE SET {update_vals} WHEN NOT MATCHED BY "
            f"TARGET THEN INSERT ({_config['insertcolumnslist']} ) VALUES ({_config['insertcolumnslist']}) ")
        print("@@@@@@@@@@ ",merge_query)
        dest_con.query(merge_query).result()
        print("@@@@@@@@@@ data copied from stage table to main table ", merge_query)
```

```python
##connection function
def get_connection(driver, connflag):
    connection_str = ""
    if (connflag == "src"):
        connection_str = (f"{_config['source_username']}:quote({_config['source_password']})@"
                          f"{_config['source_host']}:{_config['source_port']}/{_config['source_db']}")
    elif (connflag == "dest"):
        connection_str = (f"{_config['destination_username']}:quote({_config['destination_password']})@"
                          f"{_config['destination_host']}:{_config['destination_port']}/{_config['destination_db']}")
    if (driver == "mysql"):
        engine = create_engine("mysql://" + connection_str,isolation_level='AUTOCOMMIT')
    elif (driver == "postgresql"):
        engine = create_engine("postgresql://" + connection_str,isolation_level='AUTOCOMMIT')
    elif (driver == "mssql"):
        engine = create_engine("mssql+pymssql://" +connection_str,isolation_level='AUTOCOMMIT')
    elif (driver == "bigquery"):
        if(connflag=="src"):
            engine = create_engine( url= 'bigquery://',credentials_path=_config["gcp_key"])
        else:
            client = bigquery.Client()
            return client
    if (connflag == "src"):
        conn = engine.connect().execution_options(stream_results=True)
    else:
        conn = engine.connect().execution_options()
    return conn
def loadrecords():
    try:
        print("@@@@@@@@@@ Hi Job Started")
        src_driver = _config["source_driver"]
        dest_driver = _config["destination_driver"]
        src_con = get_connection(_config["source_driver"], connflag= "src")
        print("@@@@@@@@@@ connection create to" + src_driver)
        dest_con = get_connection(_config["destination_driver"], connflag= "dest")
        print("@@@@@@@@@@ connection create to" + dest_driver)
        # as we syncing every 1 minute let's put a overlapping condition to not miss any records,
        # so its last 5 minute records per minute
        condition = " WHERE " + _config["src_date_column"] + " >= NOW() - INTERVAL '5 minutes'"
        QUERY = f"select {_config['selectcolumnslist']} from {_config['source_db']}.{_config['source_table']} {condition}"
        print("@@@@@@@@@@ QUERY " + QUERY)
        count = 0
        chunk = pd.read_sql(QUERY, con=src_con, chunksize=100000)
        # First delete records from stage table
        del_query = f"DELETE FROM {_config['destination_staging_scheme']}.{_config['destination_staging_table']} WHERE 1=1"
        dest_con.query(del_query).result()
        for query_job_df in chunk:
            count = count + len(query_job_df)
            if (len(_config["src_dest_mapping"]) > 0):
                query_job_df.rename(columns=_config["src_dest_mapping"],inplace=True)
                query_job_df.rename(columns=_config["src_dest_mapping"],inplace=True)
                loc = 7  ## we want the new column to be add after 6th position
            for key, values in _config["new_columns"].items():
                query_job_df.insert(loc, key, values)
                loc = loc + 1
                table =dest_con.get_table("{}.{}.{}".format( *args _config["destination_db"],
                                                            _config["destination_schema"],
                                                            _config["destination_table_stg"]))
            dest_con.insert_rows_from_dataframe(table, query_job_df)
            print(f"@@@@@@@@@@ record count={count} " )
            ## Now that we have inserted records in to the stage table we need to merge those records into main target table
        bigquery_upsert(dest_con)
    except BaseException as e:
        traceback.print_exc()
        print("@@@@@@@@@@ scheduler completed with error ")
        exit()
    finally:
        print("@@@@@@@@@@ scheduler completed")
default_args = {'owner': 'airflow','start_date': datetime( year= 2025,  month= 1,  day= 8, tzinfo=local_tz)}
dag = DAG(_config["dag_id"], schedule_interval=_config["schedule"], default_args=default_args,catchup=False)
with dag:
    loadrecords = PythonOperator(task_id="task_id_loadrecords", python_callable=loadrecords)


loadrecords
```

Now that the airflow dag is ready, follow the steps described earlier in the book to deploy the file on airflow.

The code we developed above is a reusable template, when a new data pipeline is to be scheduled, what will change is only the _config dictionary.

10. MONITORING DATA PIPELINE

Introduction

Let's discuss in theory how the monitoring will be built and used. Sample code is not required here as it can be built using simple python API and any of the technology you are comfortable.

Now that we have developed a data pipeline and deployed it, the number of data pipelines are going to grow over time.
To manage hundreds of data pipelines we need effective monitoring and data keeping practices.

Failure of a data pipeline is not just a technical error, it may happen that a certain data pipeline's data transfer drops suddenly, which could be a logical failure at the source.

Such cases are not necessarily a failure case but can or may be a failure, so such cases must get notified and brought to the notice of the concerned team for investigation.

So we need a dashboard where we can get a snapshot view of our entire data engineering project.

Airflow by default provides a dashboard where each deployed data pipeline can be monitored.

But the airflow's dashboard caters to technical failure and success of each deployed data pipeline,the logical failures can not be judged from the airflow dashboard.

Moreover you need to open each deployed task to check for errors or to check logs through the airflow dashboard which is cumbersome, so we need a single window where we can monitor in real time.

So to monitor logical failures we need to build our own framework which gives us insight into the complete data engineering project.

Once we build it we can customize it to suit our needs.

Lets understand some of the use cases to know why we need a custom monitoring framework

Some scenarios like

Airflow is a clustered env so there could be multiple airflow servers, so the data engineering support team must know which data pipeline is deployed on which airflow server.
If a particular pipeline fails then they must know which airflow server they must login to.

A report could be required to know how many data pipelines are there from a particular database / table

Are there any duplicate data pipelines

It is possible that a certain table in source becomes unused and is not updated any more, but since the table exists the data pipeline will not fail. Such tables could be identified by checking records count of the data transferred to take further action to stop the data pipeline.

The most common information we must know to identify above scenarios is:

data pipeline metadata, i.e. _config dictionary

The duration the pipeline took to execute.

Total number of records transferred.

Error details.

Execution finished time

And we can go on adding whatever we need as per our need.

Building Blocks Of Monitoring Framework

To build our monitoring framework we need

- Database table to push the live data of the data pipeline

- API to push live data
- Integrate API into our data pipeline code

Setting Up Database Structure:

The database table would look like below, and of course we can extend it as per our need.

Below is the most basic table structure.

Column name	Type
id	bigint
filename	text
schedule	text
dag_id	text
source_driver	text
source_host	text
source_port	text
source_db	text
source_schema	text
source_table	text
source_date_column	text
selectcolumnslist	text
select_condition	text
destination_driver	text
source_date_column	text
destination_host	text
destination_port	text
destination_schema	text
destination_table	text
destination_keys	text
insertcolumnslist	text
duration	integer
filename	text
lastmodifieddate	timestamp
recordscount	integer
reference	text
schedulehh	text
schedulemm	text
select_condition	text
src_table_type	text
airflow_server	text

```
error_detailed_explaination     text
error_short_explaination        text
```

Lets us understand above table and the metadata we will maintain about each data pipeline

Apart from the columns(filename,lastmodifieddate,recordscount,duration,reference,src_table_type,airflow_server,error_short_explaination,error_short_explaination)

other columns are maintaining the static information about the data

pipeline which we defined in the _config dictionary

So let us understand the below columns which will help us in monitoring.

1. duration — This is the total duration of the execution of the data pipeline
2. filename — Python file name of the data pipeline script
3. lastmodifieddate — execution time of the data pipeline
4. recordscount — Total number of records transferred
5. reference — Here we define the need for this data pipeline, who requested,functionality and whatever is necessary
6. select_condition — data selection criteria
7. src_table_type — this source type, whether the source is a table, view or a stored procedure
8. airflow_server — description / ip of the airflow server wher we deployed this data pipeline
9. error_short_explaination — Error title
10. error_detailed_explaination — Error details

We can extend this table as per our needs

With this our meta data storage is ready to use.

Api Integration

We will need a simple REST API which will accept above information and store in the table we defined above

Let us understand the API integration part.

Let assume we have a function called **Insert_DAG_Info** which accepts the metadata and calls the API internally.

We need to build a common library as this function will be called from every data pipeline.

The signature of the functions would be like below

Insert_DAG_Info(_config,   duration,   count,
airflow_server,select_condition,
src_table_type,error_short_explaination,error_detailed_explaination,ref
erence)

All the function parameters are explained above.

duration and **count** parameter we need to calculate and pass to the function.

This function should be called at two places.
1. At the end of the data transfer loop.

       This is a scenario of successful execution of the data pipeline, so error_short_explaination,error_detailed_explaination will be sent as empty

2. In the **except** block

       This is a scenario of failure in execution of the data pipeline, so error_short_explaination,error_detailed_explaination will be sent with the error details

       Suppose our except block is like except BaseException as e:

       Then

       'error_short_explaination' would be str(e)[0:100],

       'error_detailed_explaination' would be str(e)[0:500]

Error details are big text so we will send 100 characters as short explanations and 500 characters as details, and this can be changed if required.

Monitoring Dashboard

Now we have built a monitoring database, built an API to populate the database and integrated the same in airflow tasks.

We now need a suitable dashboard which will list all the pipelines deployed on the airflow cluster and its live status.

The support team(an L1 team) will monitor the dashboard and take suitable action.

And even an ML solution can also be built which understands the behaviour of the data pipeline and raises an alert if a certain data pipeline misses the regular pattern.

11. FALLBACK MECHANISM

Our data pipelines are live and we have handled failure scenarios also.

It may still be possible that some records may get missed due to ever changing nature of the live data base and our reliance on the last modified date for data syncing.

We must make sure that in any case the data should not get missed.

We can put one fallback mechanism to make sure what ever gets missed in the incremental sync is till covered at the end of the day. We will handle this in the same job by adding one addtion scenario.

At the EoD means past midnight may be at 1 am we will sync yesterday's data,like below

```
if(datetime.now().hour==1 and datetime.now().minute < 2):
    condition = f"WHERE {_config['src_date_column']}>= DATE_TRUNC('day',NOW()-
    INTERVAL '1 days')
```

This will sync yesterday's all the record and make sure that if any of the records is missed then it will get synced at the end of the day.

12. CONCLUSION - YOUR JOURNEY FROM ZERO TO PRODUCTION AND BEYOND

Congratulations! You've reached the end of this hands-on journey through the world of data engineering. Starting with the foundational concepts, you've built a real-world data pipeline, learned about different data storage architectures, and tackled the challenges of designing for scale. This book has equipped you with the practical skills and knowledge to move data from its raw form to actionable insights.

Reflecting On Your Accomplishments

Throughout this book, you've:
Established a solid foundation: You now understand the core principles of data engineering, including data collection, storage, processing, and governance.
Mastered essential tools: You've gained experience with Python, Apache Airflow, MSSQL, PostgreSQL, MySQL, and BigQuery – technologies that are widely used in the industry.
Built a scalable data pipeline: You've designed and implemented a data pipeline capable of handling real-world data volumes and complexities.
Addressed real-world challenges: You've learned how to handle memory constraints when dealing with large datasets, how to build incremental pipelines, and how to design pipelines for different types of data sync scenarios.

The Road Ahead: Embracing The Future Of Data Engineering

The field of data engineering is constantly evolving, driven by the ever-increasing volume, velocity, and variety of data. As you continue your data engineering journey, consider these emerging trends and technologies:

Cloud-Native Data Engineering: Cloud platforms like AWS, Azure, and GCP offer a wide range of services that can simplify data engineering tasks and improve scalability. Embrace serverless architectures, managed data warehouses, and cloud-based data integration tools.

Real-Time Data Processing: The demand for real-time insights is growing. Investigate technologies like Apache Kafka, Apache Flink, and Apache Beam to build real-time data pipelines.

Your Role in Shaping the Future.

As a data engineer, you play a critical role in enabling data-driven decision-making and driving innovation. Your ability to build robust, scalable, and reliable data pipelines will empower your organization to unlock the full potential of its data.

Keep Learning, Keep Building.

The journey of a data engineer is one of continuous learning and growth. Stay curious, experiment with new technologies, and never stop building. The future of data engineering is bright, and you are now equipped to be a part of it.

..Nitin Rane..

www.ingramcontent.com/pod-product-compliance
Lightning Source LLC
LaVergne TN
LVHW041219050326
832903LV00021B/701